Anxiety

Master Your Emotions Cognitive Behavioural Therapy
For Anxiety Cognitive Behavioural Therapy Made Simple

*((Learn How To Get The Most Out Of The Herbs That Are
Proven To Fight Depression)*

Jeronimo Canales

TABLE OF CONTENT

The Cognitive And Behavioural Treatment Method 1

The Consequence Of Thinking Too Much 12

The Topic At Hand Pertains To The Examination Of Distorted Thinking Patterns.. 31

Understanding Anxiety 45

What Is The Precise Definition Of Anxiety? 49

Could You Elucidate The Contribution You Make To Others Without Explicitly Referencing Your Occupation? 62

Cognitive Disengagement From Negative Thinking 83

Interpersonal Communication In Romantic Relationships 99

The Individual Ascribes His Achievements To A Multitude Of Factors. 104

The Field Of Epidemiology Investigates The Prevalence And Determinants Of Borderline Personality Disorder.. 110

The Correlation Between Pet Ownership And Mental Well-Being 118

The Role Of Emotional Intelligence In Interpersonal Relationships 128

Cognitive Behavioural Therapy (Cbt) Encompasses A Technique Known As Thought Challenging. 132

The Process Of Disengaging From A Challenging Dialogue 147

The Cognitive And Behavioural Treatment Method

In this , we will learn what cognitive behavioural therapy (CBT) is, how it can be helpful for those who suffer from social anxiety, and what approaches can be used to control social anxiety. In addition, we will learn how CBT can be employed.

What exactly is meant by the term "cognitive behavioural therapy"?

Talk therapy is a form of cognitive behavioural therapy (CBT), which helps us confront our unhelpful thoughts and emotions and replace them with more constructive ones. In the prior , we discussed the ways in which negative attitudes and thinking processes might contribute to the development and maintenance of social anxiety. Through cognitive behavioural therapy, we are able to break out of these endless patterns. The goal of this type of treatment, which typically lasts for a shorter period of time, focuses on building healthy thought patterns that can be with us for the rest of our lives. Although the methods that we are going to go over can technically be employed by ourselves, it is always a good idea to seek the advice of a professional so that you are aware of everything that you should be doing. Even if we are able to recognise the negative thought patterns that we have, it may still be challenging to change them in the beginning without the assistance of a trained professional. Depending on what you and your therapist decide, cognitive behavioural therapy (CBT) can either be done individually or in groups.

This therapy is useful not just for social anxiety and other types of anxiety, but also for other conditions such as phobias, panic disorders, bipolar disorder, borderline personality disorder, post-traumatic stress disorder (PTSD), obsessive-compulsive disorder (OCD), psychosis, insomnia, schizophrenia, and addiction disorders. In addition to this, it may also be helpful in the management of the symptoms and pain associated with chronic fatigue syndrome, fibromyalgia, chronic pain, and irritable bowel syndrome (Overview - Cognitive Behavioural Therapy [CBT], n.d.).

The following are some of the fundamental tenets on which cognitive behavioural therapy (CBT) is based, as outlined by the American Psychological Association:

When harmful thoughts and beliefs become a regular part of your life, they can give rise to harmful behaviours, which further strengthen the negative thoughts and trap you in a vicious cycle. Emotional distress and symptoms of mental illness typically originate in the form of negative thoughts and beliefs.

● Putting these beliefs to the test and replacing them with more upbeat ideas can assist us in overcoming the challenges we confront with regard to our mental health.

Before considering whether cognitive behavioural therapy is right for you, there are a few factors you should bear in mind:

This type of therapy does not go deeply into your past problems but instead focuses on your current patterns and behaviour instead. Therefore, it is possible that it will not assist you in healing from old wounds and other traumas from the past. When it comes to social anxiety or other mental health difficulties, cognitive behavioural therapy (CBT) is not a cure, and it surely is not a fast solution. Getting go of the ideas and beliefs that have kept us going up to this point can be a difficult and time-consuming process. Your level of dedication to the therapy is an essential factor in determining how effectively cognitive behavioural therapy (CBT) sessions will work for you. You are required to collaborate with your therapist, perform your exercises on a consistent basis, and keep doing them even after your formal sessions have ended.

Cognitive behavioural therapy is focused on you and how you think about the problems and situations that you are presented with. There is more to the story than just you when it comes to social anxiety, as is the case with many other types of mental health problems. CBT is unable to assist in the resolution of those concerns.

Even while cognitive behavioural therapy (CBT) is effective, getting started with it can be a very difficult process. This is due to the fact that you first need to completely recognise all of the detrimental beliefs that are preventing you from moving forward, and then you need to actively work your way through them. This may cause you to experience a wide range of powerful feelings and may perhaps first make you feel uncomfortable.

If you want to get to the bottom of your negative patterns, you should give cognitive behavioural therapy (CBT), which is now one of the therapies that is being researched and practised the most, a go.

The Management of Stress

One definition of stress is "any physical, physiological, or emotional condition that creates bodily or mental disturbance and that may play a role in producing illness." Stress can be defined as any condition that creates bodily or mental disturbance.

Trauma, infections, poisons, diseases, and injuries of any kind are all examples of physical and chemical factors that have the potential to produce stress.

There is a wide range of emotional material that might serve as a trigger for stress and anxiety.

The term "stress" is used by scientists and clinicians to designate any force that disrupts the stability and balance of a person's physical functioning. Many people associate the word "stress" with the psychological stress that they experience.

If stress disrupts the homeostasis and function of the body, does that mean that all stress is bad? Certainly not in every case. On occasion, a moderate amount of stress and worry could prove to be beneficial.

For instance, when we are in the middle of completing a project or task, it is common for us to feel anxious. This feeling typically motivates us to perform well, concentrate more intently, and work more diligently.

In a similar vein, physical activity may place transient strain on a number of physiological systems, but the benefits to one's health are abundantly clear. It is only when stress is allowed to build up to a high level or when it is poorly managed that its negative effects become apparent.

One of the most important goals for people who are stressed is to gain control over the pressures of their lives. Because of the inevitable nature of stress in everyday life, it is impossible to completely rid oneself of it.

It is difficult to completely get rid of stress, and doing so probably wouldn't be a good idea either. Instead, we should learn different methods of stress management, such as relaxation techniques and other approaches, so that we can exert more control over our stress and the negative effects it has on our physical and mental health.

Self-Monitoring: Self-monitoring is defined as the process of observing and recording one's own thoughts, feelings, and behaviours in relation to anxiety-inducing situations or triggers.

The Importance of Carrying Out Self-Monitoring: Self-monitoring is the cornerstone of cognitive behavioural therapy (CBT) due to the insight it provides into the cycles and stimuli that cause anxiety. It assists people in becoming more aware of their own internal experiences and how those experiences relate to anxiety symptoms.

Techniques for One's Own Self-Monitoring: Individuals who suffer from anxiety are frequently encouraged by their therapists to keep a journal or use smartphone apps to keep track of their thoughts, feelings, and behaviours. When it comes to recognising patterns and triggers that contribute to anxiety, this can be an especially helpful strategy.

Benefits for the Alleviation of Anxiety: Individuals who engage in self-monitoring are able to: Recognise recurrent thought patterns and cognitive distortions that contribute to anxiety.

Gain an understanding of the specific circumstances or settings that bring on feelings of anxiety.

Monitor their progression over time as they put CBT strategies into practise.

Cognitive distortions are patterns of thinking that are inaccurate and have a tendency to reinforce negative emotions such as anxiety. Other names for cognitive distortions include thinking errors and irrational beliefs.

Common Cognitive Errors There are many different types of cognitive errors that are common, including the following:

Nothing but the Whole Pie Thinking: Seeing things as being either completely positive or completely negative.

Catastrophizing means to anticipate the most negative outcome possible.

An example of overgeneralization would be drawing broad, unfavourable conclusions based on a small amount of evidence.

Personalization is when someone blames themselves for things that happened to them outside of themselves.

Individuals are taught to question their own thought processes as part of cognitive behavioural therapy (CBT), which helps people recognise the cognitive distortions they may be experiencing. Individuals learn to evaluate the accuracy and validity of their negative thoughts, rather than simply accepting them at face value.

Benefits for the Treatment of Anxiety One of the most important steps in the process of alleviating anxiety is recognising and addressing any cognitive distortions that may be present. It is possible for individuals to replace irrational beliefs with thoughts that are more balanced and rational through the process of recognising and correcting distorted thinking. This can result in decreased anxiety and improved emotional well-being.

The Consequence Of Thinking Too Much

1. Excessive rumination has the potential to contribute to the development of hypertension, as those who engage in overthinking are more prone to experiencing elevated blood pressure levels. The brain experiences physiological stress during episodes of excessive rumination, which might potentially lead to a progressive elevation in blood pressure. Hypertension is a perilous condition that can lead to fatal cardiovascular complications or other significant health issues. It is advisable to have regular blood pressure assessments in instances where one experiences numerous episodes of overthinking, as this might facilitate the acquisition of self-help techniques. Blood pressure can be regulated through the consumption of specific dietary choices.

2. The act of excessively studying or scrutinizing can negatively impact one's desire to eat.

Overthinking can also have an affect on one's eating behavior. In the event that one refrains from consuming food as a means to suppress their hunger, they may choose to abstain from meals for consecutive days. Consequently, individuals may encounter significant and detrimental reductions in body weight that are deemed medically unsound.

The act of excessively analyzing and overthinking can induce feelings of anxiety, as it serves as a stress reaction when engaged in regularly. Manifestations of worry in the physical realm encompass a range of observable indicators such as quivering hands, profuse perspiration, difficulty in swallowing, respiratory distress, and various other associated manifestations.

The act of excessively analyzing or overthinking can disrupt one's ability to sleep, hence having a detrimental impact on the individual's sleep patterns. Your sleep schedule can be impacted, and you might wake up feeling exhausted. Moreover, it is worth noting that individuals may find themselves endeavoring to engage in sleep during periods when they should be engaging in work or physical activity. This phenomenon would impact an individual's daily routine and result in a persistent manifestation of physical exhaustion.

The act of overthinking leads to the depletion of cognitive resources, resulting in a state of mental fatigue. Upon devoting one's cognitive and physical resources to a particular concern, an individual may experience a sense of emotional depletion by day's end. This phenomenon has the potential to diminish one's interest in various subjects that would otherwise be captivating. Participating in routine activities such as grocery shopping or engaging in casual conversations can be mentally and physically draining, potentially resulting in a depletion of energy reserves that may hinder engagement in other tasks or activities. In isolation, the act of overthinking does not possess the status of a formally acknowledged mental disorder. Nevertheless, empirical research has demonstrated that it commonly presents itself as an indicator of comorbid mental health disorders, including but not limited to depression and various anxiety problems.

Obsessive-compulsive disorder (OCD) and post-traumatic stress disorder (PTSD) are two psychological conditions that will be discussed in this paper. Post-traumatic stress disorder (PTSD) is a psychological condition that can develop in those who have experienced or seen a traumatic event.

Research suggests that there is a mutual dependence between stress and overthinking. The tendency to engage in excessive thinking can be intensified by elevated levels of stress, worry, and melancholy. Excessive rumination, in the interim, has the potential to exacerbate levels of stress, anxiety, and despondency. It is customary to exhibit hypervigilance following a distressing event, characterized by a heightened state of alertness and constant vigilance for potential threats. Hypervigilance is perceived by certain persons as an exaggerated concern for potential indicators of concern.

The act of overthinking or engaging in excessive cognitive processes can be mentally and physically draining. The phenomenon has the potential to deplete individuals of their emotional and physical vitality, thereby resulting in a wastage of human emotional resources. The act of overthinking, or engaging in excessive cognitive processes, has a detrimental impact on human beings, leading to a diminished capacity for effective decision-making. Moreover, it has the potential to impede our progress and heighten our susceptibility to experiencing anxiety. Additionally, it has the potential to induce nocturnal awakenings or hinder the onset of sleep. Excessive emotional arousal may result in heightened emotional reactivity, increased susceptibility to anger, and difficulties in maintaining concentration and focus. Excessive rumination or hypercognition can result in a significant allocation of time towards internal contemplation.

In the presence of others, we tend to exhibit a lack of emotional engagement. It is possible for someone to perceive a lack of interest in the subject matter being discussed, as they may interpret our preoccupation with personal ideas as a diversion of attention away from the individual with whom we are engaged in conversation. Moreover, this could have negative implications for our interpersonal connections. Overanalyzing can serve as a cognitive approach aimed at assuming agency over a given situation and cultivating a heightened sense of autonomy in determining subsequent actions. During episodes of excessive rumination, the brain engages in the process of generating and evaluating potential situations, so facilitating the formation of predictions with the aim of inducing a state of calmness. Consequently, individuals often find themselves in this particular condition and have difficulties in progressing and initiating action. When individuals engage in excessive rumination, their cognitive processes tend to create additional inquiries that pertain to potential sources of concern. It has been found that certain individuals may engage in rumination more frequently than others. For example, those with perfectionistic tendencies exhibit a higher susceptibility to engaging in excessive rumination. Perfectionists and overachievers often engage in a process of self-evaluation and self-critique due to their strong desire for flawlessness and aversion to failure. The two primary elements underlying overthinking are stress and worry. Additional factors that frequently contribute to overthinking are issues related to an individual's self-esteem and feelings of self-doubt. The phenomenon of stress and anxiety has been shown to arise as a consequence of social withdrawal, a behavior that has become prevalent due to the ongoing epidemic. Anxiety is an often seen response to feelings of apprehension. The concerns over our future have been amplified due to the ongoing epidemic and the multitude of uncertainties associated with several elements, such as health conditions, mortality rates, and economic stability. These conditions have led us to engage in extensive contemplation. Fear is identified as one of the primary factors contributing to the widespread occurrence of overthinking among individuals. Individuals who experience fear frequently engage in rumination, fixating on their concerns and directing their attention towards the most pessimistic potential outcomes. This phenomenon might potentially lead to a self-perpetuating loop of negative thinking, hindering one's ability to focus on positive outcomes.

The comprehension of anxiety

Anxiety is a psychological condition characterized by the presence of emotional states marked by emotions of apprehension, uneasiness, or distress in relation to a situation or circumstance that is accompanied by an unclear conclusion. Stress is a common occurrence in human existence and can serve as a beneficial factor in specific contexts, such as prior to a significant examination or employment evaluation.

Nevertheless, in cases where anxiety reaches an excessive level and disrupts one's regular functioning, it could potentially indicate the presence of an anxiety disorder. This refers to a state characterized by persistent and overpowering emotions of anxiety and worry, which impede one's ability to engage in typical daily activities.

The present discourse aims to elucidate the concept of anxiety, a psychological phenomenon characterized by feelings of apprehension, unease, and

Anxiety disorders encompass a collection of mental health illnesses characterized by the presence of heightened and enduring emotions of fear, apprehension, and restlessness. These emotions may be accompanied by physiological manifestations such as elevated heart rate, perspiration, and muscular tension.

There exist various classifications of anxiety disorders, encompassing generalized anxiety disorder (GAD), panic disorder, social anxiety disorder, and specific phobias. Every category possesses its own distinct array of symptoms and available treatment modalities.

Various Forms of Anxiety Disorders

Generalized anxiety disorder (GAD) is distinguished by the presence of chronic and disproportionate apprehension for routine matters, such as employment, well-being, or familial relationships. Individuals diagnosed with Generalized Anxiety Disorder (GAD) may encounter challenges in managing their excessive worrying tendencies, often experiencing feelings of anxiety even in the absence of any tangible or imminent danger.

Panic disorder is characterized by the occurrence of repeated panic attacks, which are abrupt periods of heightened terror accompanied by physiological manifestations such as chest discomfort and respiratory distress.

Social anxiety disorder, sometimes referred to as social phobia, is characterized by an intense apprehension about social interactions and a heightened dread of being scrutinized or assessed by others. Individuals with this illness may encounter challenges when attempting to participate in routine activities,

Logical-mathematical intelligence, although important, possesses limitations. Moreover, there are even moral and in some cases legal problems related to IQ testing -a test that is administered to volunteers to derive information about their logical-mathematical intelligence. Let's look at these issues related to the limits of rationality.

First, there is the possibility of creating a negative bias toward other forms of intelligence. For example, intelligence related to the more creative and artistic fields might be penalized when purely logical and rational types of intelligence are exalted too much. Hence, it is imperative to critically reassess the evaluative framework employed at the school level, with regards to the assessment of boys and girls, in order to ensure that all individuals can attain contentment and social acknowledgement in accordance with their respective aptitudes. The disparity in the assessment of intelligence between an exceptional and very talented musician and a mathematician is deemed unjust.

Furthermore, it is important to note that logical intelligence does not bear any resemblance to the capacity to comprehend and empathize with the emotions and sentiments of individuals. Nevertheless, the capacity to establish emotional connections with individuals is inherently crucial in human existence. Consequently, it is plausible that society as a whole would derive advantages from an educational framework that acknowledges the significance of human emotions. Living in a culture that prioritizes persons who possess harsh but proficient abstract reasoning skills above those who demonstrate empathy and attentive listening abilities might be seen unjust.

Ultimately, the extent of logical-mathematical intelligence may be constrained by external variables that are not subject to personal influence, such as illnesses and challenges associated with the progression of aging. As individuals progress through the aging process, there is a potential reduction in their cognitive capacity to answer mathematical problems. Likewise, certain medical conditions, such as Alzheimer's disease, can have a detrimental impact on an individual's cognitive functions, namely their logical thinking and problem-solving capabilities.

At present, I would want to expound upon the constraints and ethical concerns pertaining to intelligence quotient (IQ) assessments. The assessments are derived from the delivery of examinations that solely evaluate individuals' capacity to solve problems pertaining to abstract reasoning. In addition, the assessments allocate a quantitative measure, specifically referred to as the Intelligence Quotient (IQ), to an individual's cognitive intelligence. Nevertheless, it is imperative to consider that these assessments are formulated by individuals who may possess dissimilar characteristics and undoubtedly harbor prejudices or fundamental ideas that diverge from our own. The issue at hand is to the inequity of assessing individuals solely on the basis of their profound and firmly entrenched convictions.

The topic of personal relationships is of great significance and has been widely studied in various academic disciplines. It encompasses the study of interpersonal connections

One of the most prominent and intricate consequences of anxious attachment manifests in interpersonal relationships. The capacity to significantly impact the nature of one's close interpersonal connections, often leading to intricate dynamics, is evident.

The constant need for reassurance is a common characteristic observed in individuals with anxiety, who often seek continuing validation and reinforcement of affection and commitment within their interpersonal interactions. Both individuals involved in the partnership may encounter emotional strain and fatigue as a consequence of this situation.

- The Fear of Abandonment: The apprehension of abandonment is a central theme within the context of anxious attachment. When a partner experiences periods of separation, it is possible for them to develop feelings of anxiety, leading to behaviors characterized by excessive attachment and a desire to exert control.

- Jealousy and Insecurity: The phenomenon of jealousy often emerges as a recurring theme within partnerships characterized by anxious attachment. Envy and distrust are commonly experienced by individuals, often manifesting in the form of mental imagery depicting pessimistic outcomes.

- Challenges Associated with limits: Individuals with anxious attachment tendencies may encounter obstacles when attempting to build and sustain healthy limits. Individuals could encounter difficulties in discerning instances where they encroach upon their partner's personal boundaries or infringe upon their emotional independence.

The dynamics of relationships involving individuals with anxiety can be characterized by heightened intensity, marked by rapid shifts between expressions of affection and devotion, and feelings of unease and emotional distress. Both individuals involved in the partnership may encounter emotional fatigue due to these fluctuations.

The Topic At Hand Pertains To The Examination Of Distorted Thinking Patterns.

When individuals experience anxiety, it frequently originates from the presence of amplified negative cognitions that rapidly traverse their thoughts. These cognitive distortions involve the tendency to jump to the most negative outcomes, generalize excessively, or make unfounded predictions. The identification and mitigation of erroneous ideas play a crucial role in the effective management of anxiety.

Cognitive behavioral therapy (CBT) employs the principle of recognizing and substituting erroneous thoughts. The initial stage involves the recognition of instances where thinking influenced by fear emerges. What are the common situations that elicit feelings of anxiety? Please record the information in written form.

Subsequently, it is necessary to undertake a comprehensive analysis of cognitive processes in an impartial manner, while also questioning their soundness and credibility. Inquire about the rationality of this concern, whether it is grounded in reality or if it is an instance of catastrophizing. Is it possible that I am making unfavorable assumptions about the motives of others without sufficient evidence? Are there any alternative perspectives that I may not have considered?

Collect empirical data to evaluate apprehensive conjectures. To illustrate, it is advisable to develop a systematic approach, such as an action plan, while investigating a health risk, rather than engaging in speculative conjectures without substantial evidence. Frequently, viable and optimistic options exist that surpass the most dire scenario.

Substitute cognitive distortions with rational viewpoints based on logical reasoning. For instance, the statement "everything is ruined" can be reframed as "this situation represents a setback, however, it presents an opportunity for personal growth and eventual restoration."

Engage in repeated iterations of this procedure, ensuring to engage in discussions pertaining to it with a counselor.

Developing the ability to retrain anxious thought patterns requires a significant level of dedication. However, over time, this cognitive practice becomes more robust, thereby diminishing the influence of worry by counteracting the distorting effects of negative self-talk.

Now, let us delve into prevalent cognitive distortions and examine techniques to mitigate their impact.

Catastrophizing refers to the cognitive tendency of individuals to anticipate and magnify the occurrence of the most unfavorable outcome, while also amplifying the potential negative consequences associated with it. Presenting evidence regarding the diminished likelihood of peril.

• Dichotomous Thinking - Perceiving results as either absolute successes or failures, without considering any intermediate possibilities.

Examine the potential good aspects within setbacks.

Overgeneralization refers to the tendency to draw broad and negative judgments based on a single experience. Reflect about previous instances that contradict the current argument or hypothesis.

• Divination - Anticipating unfavorable consequences without empirical substantiation. Counteract pessimistic forecasts by presenting alternative scenarios that are more probable.

• Labeling - Employing hyperbolic language such as "loser" or "failure" in a broad and sweeping manner. Substitute generic terms with precise and quantifiable descriptions.

Emotional reasoning refers to the cognitive process of assuming that emotions accurately reflect objective reality, hence treating subjective sentiments as factual evidence. Examine and evaluate apprehensions related to tests in light of empirical evidence.

• Should Statements - Imposing inflexible regulations upon oneself that establish impractical benchmarks. It is suggested to relax the regulations pertaining to the use of the word "should" and instead consider adopting a more flexible approach by using the phrase "it would be desirable if..."

Discounting positives refers to the tendency to dismiss or downplay positive experiences or outcomes as either inconsequential or mere instances of luck. Maintain a gratitude diary to record daily instances of positivity.

The phenomenon of mind reading involves the tendency to make assumptions about the negative motivations of others without sufficient empirical evidence. Enumerate alternative benign motivations.

- The cognitive bias of magnification and minimization involves the tendency to overemphasize issues or negative aspects while downplaying or reducing strengths or positive aspects. It is important to adopt a balanced approach that takes into account both the challenges and capabilities involved.

The identification of cognitive patterns

Social anxiety frequently include cognitive distortions that exacerbate feelings of anxiety. Gaining an understanding of these cognitive patterns is crucial for the successful implementation of appropriate coping methods.

Individuals with social anxiety often exhibit a cognitive tendency known as catastrophic thinking, wherein they habitually participate in the process of envisioning and dwelling upon the most severe and unfavorable outcomes within social contexts. When an individual becomes aware of their tendency to engage in catastrophizing, it is advisable to counteract these thoughts by employing more balanced and realistic perspectives.

The Phenomenon of Mind Reading: Socially anxious individuals often assume they know what others are thinking about them, usually assuming negative judgments. Engage in the process of critically examining these assumptions and explore alternate perspectives that may offer more optimistic readings of how people perceive things.

Self-criticism is the act of evaluating one's own actions, behaviors, or performance It is vital to direct one's focus towards their self-talk. Do you have a tendency towards self-criticism? The cultivation of self-compassion is crucial in the effective management of social anxiety. Substitute self-critique with self-affirmation and self-compassion.

Requesting Expert Evaluation

While self-assessment is a valuable starting point, consider seeking professional assessment and diagnosis. A mental health practitioner, such as a therapist or psychiatrist, possesses the expertise to conduct a comprehensive assessment of your social anxiety, provide specialized perspectives, and assist in the formulation of an individualized intervention strategy.

Establishing Objectives for Personal Development

Following the acquisition of knowledge and understanding through self-evaluation and self-consciousness, it becomes imperative to establish precise objectives for personal enhancement.

Commence with a modest approach: It is advisable to commence by setting attainable and less daunting objectives that effectively test your anxiety levels. As one's confidence grows, it is advisable to incrementally elevate the level of intricacy associated with their ambitions.

The concept of SMART goals is widely recognized and utilized in various fields, including business, education, and personal development. SMART is an To ensure the effectiveness of your goals, it is recommended to adhere to the SMART framework, which stands for Specific, Measurable, Achievable, Relevant, and Time-bound. This framework guarantees that one's objectives are unambiguous, achievable, and concentrated.

The monitoring and assessment of progress. It is advisable to maintain a comprehensive log of both accomplishments and obstacles encountered. It is imperative to acknowledge and commemorate one's achievements, regardless of their magnitude, while also deriving valuable lessons from any encountered obstacles.

Request Assistance: It is advisable to communicate your aspirations to a reliable confidant, such as a trusted friend, family member, or therapist, who can offer support, empathy, and a sense of responsibility.

The integration of self-assessment, heightened self-awareness, and goal-setting establishes a robust framework for effectively managing and ultimately surmounting social anxiety. In the subsequent s, an extensive array of ideas and techniques will be examined to assist individuals in effectively maneuvering social settings with heightened self-assurance and proficiency.

Misconceptions Regarding Anxiety and Depression

Let us go into prevalent myths and misconceptions around anxiety and depression that are currently circulating. The current situation might be likened to a setting characterized by a multitude of circulating hearsay, necessitating an endeavor to illuminate the veracity of the matter at hand.

One common misconception is the belief that individuals can simply "snap out of" their mental health struggles.

Instances arise in which individuals assert the notion of "simply adopting a positive mindset," implying the ability to instantaneously alleviate feelings of worry or depression, akin to the act of turning off a light switch. Herein lies the veracity assessment—these circumstances do not exhibit a binary nature akin to the operation of a light switch. It is not feasible to instantaneously eliminate them by simply snapping one's fingers. These sensations are genuine and intricate, encompassing both cognitive and physiological aspects. Consider the scenario of instructing a fractured bone to undergo self-repair without the aid of medical intervention; such a proposition proves to be far from straightforward.

Myth Two: The phenomenon is solely a product of psychological factors.

Indeed, anxiety and depression are intricately linked to cognitive and emotional processes, however their impact extends beyond the realm of one's mental faculties. These covert individuals possess the ability to manipulate the human body in a collaborative manner. The physiological parameters of heart rate, sleep patterns, and energy levels are all included in the list of variables under consideration. When someone dismiss a condition as merely psychological, it is appropriate to inform them that it is better understood as a comprehensive orchestration involving the entire body.

Myth Three: "Depression and anxiety are exclusively experienced by individuals lacking strength or resilience."

Let us thoroughly debunk this prevalent misconception. The notion that individuals who contract a cold are exclusively those who are perceived as "weak" is a concept worth contemplating. This assertion appears to be lacking in logical coherence, does it not? Mental health conditions exhibit similarities. Discrimination based on strength or character is not practiced by them. Indeed, individuals can be impacted by these factors, irrespective of their perceived resilience or outward appearance. Therefore, it is imperative to discard this fallacious belief and instead acknowledge the veracity that soliciting assistance and pursuing support necessitates a considerable amount of fortitude.

Myth Four: "The ability to discern signs of depression or anxiety in individuals is always present."

It is akin to making the assumption that one can consistently identify a superhero amidst a gathering of individuals, however, this presumption is not entirely accurate. The manifestation of mental health challenges is not always overtly conspicuous. Individuals possess the ability to adeptly conceal their internal struggles beneath expressions of joy and amusement. Merely seeming outwardly unaffected does not necessarily imply the absence of personal struggles. Occasionally, individuals exhibiting exceptional strength are those who engage in combat against imperceptible adversaries.

Myth Five: "Pharmaceutical intervention is the sole remedy"

Consider the following analogy: envision a comprehensive toolkit with several tactics designed to effectively address and mitigate symptoms of anxiety and sadness. Pharmaceutical intervention may constitute a singular component within the aforementioned repertoire, although it does not exclusively encompass the entirety of available options. Therapeutic interventions, practices of self-care, networks of support, and modifications to one's lifestyle collectively comprise the array of strategies available for individuals seeking to address their well-being. Similar to constructing a dwelling, the effective management of one's mental well-being necessitates the utilization of a diverse range of strategies.

These myths are hereby debunked. The unveiling of prevalent misunderstandings around anxiety and depression has allowed for a deeper understanding of their underlying truths. In this endeavor, it is crucial to recognize that possessing comprehension and empathy can serve as advantageous attributes. It is imperative to maintain a continuous pursuit of knowledge by persistently posing inquiries, while concurrently extending support to individuals who may encounter such obstacles. Collectively, we possess the capacity to reframe the narrative and construct a society in which misconceptions surrounding mental health are rendered obsolete.

Understanding Anxiety

This provides an elucidation of the nature of light, the various manifestations it can assume, and its influence on the daily lives of individuals. In addition, our efforts will be directed towards mitigating the societal stigma surrounding anxiety, emphasizing its prevalence as a ubiquitous human emotional experience.

What is the precise definition of anxiety?

Anxiety is a prevalent psychological response shown in individuals when faced with situations of stress or perceived threat. The physiological response of experiencing butterflies in the stomach prior to a significant presentation or the cognitive phenomenon of racing thoughts that disrupt sleep due to apprehension over an impending event are common occurrences. Anxiety can be understood as a physiological response that primes the body to confront a perceived threat.

While this response may yield advantages in some circumstances, such as when faced with a genuine danger, it can prove disadvantageous when it occurs excessively or with heightened intensity. Anxiety disorders can be identified when anxiety persists and hampers daily functioning.

Various Types of Anxiety Disorders

The manifestation of anxiety is not uniform and varies among individuals. There exists a diverse range of anxiety disorders, each characterized by distinct qualities and symptoms. Some of the most commonly occurring anxiety disorders include:

Generalized Anxiety Disorder (GAD) is characterized by individuals experiencing excessive worry and anxiety throughout various domains of their lives, often lacking a discernible precipitating factor.

2. Social anxiety disorder: This disorder is defined by an excessive level of anxiety pertaining to social interactions, accompanied by a concern regarding the evaluation or scrutiny of one's behavior by others.

Panic disorder is distinguished by the presence of recurrent and unforeseen panic attacks, which manifest as intense episodes of anxiety followed by physiological manifestations such as elevated heart rate and respiratory distress.

4. Specific Phobias: These are irrational anxieties pertaining to a singular object

or situation, such as acrophobia (fear of heights), arachnophobia (fear of spiders), or aviophobia (fear of flying).

Compulsive-Compulsive Disorder (OCD) is a psychological condition that is distinguished by the presence of intrusive thoughts and the engagement in repetitive behaviors or rituals aimed at alleviating anxiety.

6. Posttraumatic Stress Disorder (PTSD): PTSD emerges subsequent to the experience of a traumatic event and is distinguished by manifestations like intrusive recollections, distressing dreams, and heightened states of anxiety.

Gaining a comprehensive comprehension of the inherent characteristics of one's anxiety constitutes the initial phase in effectively managing and regulating it. It is important to acknowledge that one's experience of anxiety is not an isolated occurrence, since there exists a substantial global population grappling with similar mental health challenges.

What Is The Precise Definition Of Anxiety?

Anxiety transcends the realm of a rudimentary emotion or fleeting concern. The aforementioned mental state possesses a profound and pervasive nature, exerting its influence on individuals in diverse manners. In order to gain a comprehensive understanding of anxiety, it is necessary to thoroughly explore its many aspects, encompassing its physiological, psychological, and emotional elements.

Anxiety, fundamentally, is an innate physiological reaction ingrained within the human biological framework. The heightened level of alertness and attentiveness observed in individuals has developed over an extended period of time as an adaptive mechanism for survival. In response to perceived threats, the human body initiates the release of stress hormones, including as cortisol and adrenaline, which serve to prime individuals for a physiological reaction commonly referred to as the "fight or flight" response. This instinctive response facilitated our predecessors in efficiently confronting physical hazards.

Nevertheless, in contemporary society, worry frequently presents itself in distinct ways. The phenomenon of stress has evolved beyond being only a reaction to urgent physical dangers, and can now arise from a diverse range of origins, including financial concerns, societal expectations, or existential inquiries. The transition from acute anxiety, which is focused on immediate survival, to chronic anxiety, which is often characterized by unreasonable fear, exemplifies the intricate nature of this emotional state.

Anxiety is characterized by a series of physiological alterations throughout the body. The cardiovascular system exhibits an increased heart rate, while the musculoskeletal system has heightened muscle tension, and the respiratory system demonstrates accelerated breathing. These responses can be considered as vestiges of our evolutionary legacy, priming us for potential action. Nevertheless, in cases when anxiety becomes chronic or disproportionate in relation to the perceived threat, it can give rise to a variety of bodily manifestations, encompassing symptoms such as headaches and gastrointestinal disturbances.

Anxiety exerts a psychological impact on our cognitive processes and perceptual experiences. The phenomenon has the potential to distort our perception, leading to an increased sensitivity towards prospective threats and an inclination to magnify even trivial concerns. The presence of a skewed lens has the potential to initiate a recurring pattern of rumination, whereby worrisome thoughts persistently circulate, thereby exacerbating the emotional distress.

Anxiety is a psychological state characterized by a profound sense of unease and fear. The phenomenon has the capacity to elicit a feeling of imminent catastrophe, apprehension, or even extreme fear. The experience of emotional turbulence is frequently accompanied by a deep feeling of powerlessness, as individuals struggle with ideas and sensations that are beyond their ability to manage.

It is imperative to acknowledge that anxiety is a heterogeneous phenomenon, and hence cannot be universally characterized or understood. The phenomenon in question has a range of manifestations, spanning from a slight sense of discomfort to more pronounced pathological conditions. Generalized Anxiety Disorder (GAD), Social Anxiety Disorder, and Panic Disorder represent a subset of conditions characterized by the prominence of anxiety, which exerts a substantial influence on individuals' everyday functioning.

Anxiety is known to flourish in situations characterized by uncertainty. The apprehension towards unfamiliar circumstances can serve as a fertile environment for the development of anxious cognitions, and this lack of assurance can encompass both individual problems and broader world issues. The contemporary society, characterized by an incessant influx of information and a quick tempo, has the potential to intensify this feeling of uneasiness.

Anxiety can be understood as a complex interplay of biological, psychological, and emotional factors. The survival mechanism has become dysfunctional when confronted with the intricacies of modern society. The comprehensive comprehension of anxiety's extensive impact on our lives necessitates the acknowledgment of its physiological, psychological, and emotional dimensions. This condition necessitates the cultivation of empathy, heightened awareness, and the implementation of efficient coping mechanisms in order to navigate the complex interplay it creates within the realm of human existence.

6: The Intersection of Psychology and the Crisis of Anxiety: Unveiling Unexplored Aspects.

Individuals who lack prior experience with therapy, or those who are actively engaged in treatment, may possess a limited comprehension of the underlying mechanisms via which this discipline facilitates the management of anxiety and other pathological conditions. This aims to elucidate the advantages and mechanisms underlying the phenomena under investigation.

Psychotherapy is widely regarded as a highly effective intervention for addressing emotional disorders. Irrespective of the underlying cause, such as anxiety attacks or other related concerns, the involvement of a psychologist in facilitating these changes holds significant importance.

The comprehension of causality under various circumstances, particularly during periods of solitude and emotional distress, is a rare occurrence. The difficulty arises from the fact that upon awakening, we assume a seated position without comprehending the subject matter at hand.

There is a frequent inquiry regarding the significance of employing an expert inside a particular domain. Consider a scenario where an individual is confronted with the necessity of traversing a bridge, although harboring an indeterminate phobia of heights. In this particular circumstance, there exists no alternative means of transportation, hence rendering the act of crossing imperative. Would it be advantageous to have a companion that provides physical support and guidance, assisting you in traversing a path when you see yourself to be unable of continuing further? Engaging the services of a psychologist or other specialized expert entails having a supportive someone to provide guidance during times of overwhelming adversity.

Engaging in discussions with friends regarding personal anguish can provide a sense of solace, as having a receptive listener can be comforting. However, it is important to note that the manner in which these individuals lend an ear is often rooted in their personal life experiences rather than professional expertise. Hence, it is frequently posited that our experiences of pain are typically dismissed as subjective or psychosomatic in nature. The individuals in question acquired knowledge via their experiences, yet failed to grasp the concept that one should not endure suffering in isolation. Moreover, they remained unaware that engaging in discussions about their hardships does not diminish their personal strength or character. The identification of individuals upon whom one may rely is crucial in order to prevent exacerbation of circumstances.

With whom have you been engaged in conversation?

There exist those who possess a desire to acquire knowledge regarding ongoing events, either driven by mere curiosity or with the intention of engaging in casual conversation with the first individual they encounter, pertaining to your personal experiences and suffering. This is the reason why there exist professionals who dedicate years to studying in order to acquire the expertise necessary to effectively listen to individuals while also providing them with strategies to combat this malevolent force. It is important to recognize that there is a distinct difference between hearing and actively engaging in the process of listening. Psychology, as an empirical discipline, offers a range of well-established strategies that have been developed over time to effectively address mental health concerns.

Normal anxiety has a crucial role in ensuring our survival. This compels individuals to venture beyond their comfort zones and actively pursue optimal outcomes. Pathological anxiety, also known as excessive anxiety, refers to anxiety experienced at heightened levels that significantly impairs an individual's daily functioning. This condition manifests as an overwhelming sense of worry, leading to the amplification of seemingly little matters into formidable challenges that are arduous to manage.

It often becomes challenging for individuals to independently ascertain the extent of their worry. Alternatively, one may ascertain the presence of a pathological condition. Consider a scenario in which one finds oneself in an abusive relationship. It can be challenging for individuals involved in such a relationship to recognize the presence of disharmony and toxicity, which depletes their energy reserves.

Perhaps you have experienced a connection of this nature. Nevertheless, individuals who lack any personal attachment and approach situations solely from a rational standpoint possess the ability to discern anomalies. Similar to individuals who experience anxiety, upon recognizing the presence of the disorder, they have already endured numerous sleepless nights and have encountered significant disruptions to their mental well-being.

Psychotherapy facilitates the exploration of one's inner self, enabling a comprehensive understanding of the underlying origins of anxiety episodes. The individual engages in a process of introspection, wherein they actively examine the underlying causes and consciously evaluate the stimuli in collaboration with the therapist. In typical circumstances, individuals may not readily recognize the presence of crises stemming from a particular traumatic event, such as one experienced during adolescence, which thereafter manifests in recurring and increasingly acute episodes.

Individuals who have not previously engaged in treatment may possess a natural inclination to inquire about the activities and occurrences that transpire within the confines of a therapy session, often lasting for a duration of fifty minutes. This discourse aims to present an alternative perspective on the topic of treatment, highlighting its merits and dispelling common misconceptions around its efficacy.

During the initial 0 to 10 minutes, the user expresses a lack of conversational topics for the present day.

Within a time frame of 10 to 20 minutes, the individual engages in the act of expressing various topics in a completely arbitrary manner.

Within a time frame of 30 to 40 minutes, the individual engages in a process of self-discovery, wherein they uncover and explore past traumas, so gaining a deeper understanding of their own identity.

During a duration of approximately 40 to 50 minutes, it is highly likely that one will have emotional responses such as shedding tears or exclaiming the word "nooossa" on multiple occasions.

In the span of 60 minutes, individuals engage in the act of bidding farewell, experiencing positive emotions, and expressing a desire for subsequent sessions.

Could You Elucidate The Contribution You Make To Others Without Explicitly Referencing Your Occupation?

This will provide an examination of the disparities between the Western interpretation of Ikigai and its conventional Japanese connotation.

There exist some prevalent misconceptions surrounding the concept of Ikigai that warrant clarification.

Strategies for cultivating one's Ikigai in the absence of a discovered interest.

The concept of Imperfect Ikigai refers to the notion that one's sense of purpose and fulfillment in life may not always align

Only a small minority of individuals possess the capability to consistently attain complete Ikigai across all domains of their existence. That is acceptable. It is possible that individuals may lack enthusiasm or passion towards their occupation or other facets of their daily regimen. The acquisition and refinement of skills and talents may remain vital in order to attain one's desired position or status in life. It is possible that one may not be leading a lifestyle characterized by optimal balance, wherein their Ikigai is consistently and fully engaged. It is important to bear in mind that Ikigai pertains to the process or trajectory of attaining a life imbued with significance, rather than solely focusing on the ultimate outcome. Hence, one's Ikigai perpetually exhibits an inherent incompleteness, as life itself is an ongoing and evolving endeavor. Regardless of the seeming distance from attaining one's Ikigai, it is imperative to maintain the awareness that this intrinsic life purpose cannot be forfeited, as it constitutes the fundamental essence of one's being. Through the passage of time and personal development, the revelation of one's Ikigai shall inevitably occur.

Even individuals who possess a firmly developed Ikigai may nevertheless experience unfavorable circumstances on certain days. Individuals may continue to experience certain aspects of their lives that elicit feelings of dissatisfaction. One will always encounter instances of failure. As a result of many situations, frequently beyond one's control, it may be observed that achieving complete integration of Ikigai into every aspect of one's daily life is not always feasible. That is acceptable. Please exert your best effort. Having some is preferable to having none. It is acceptable to not get optimal outcomes in every attempt at batting. Doubles, singles, bunts, and walks are all acceptable methods of advancing in the game. In the event that one fails to make contact with the ball during a swing or hits a foul ball, it is worth noting that the individual remains in the batting position.

When experiencing discouragement in the pursuit of discovering one's Ikigai, it is advisable to transform the term into a verb. Consider your Ikigai as a catalyst for action, motivating and guiding your endeavors. In alternative terms, an individual's Ikigai may encompass activities involving creation, construction, acquisition of knowledge, exertion of influence, or manifestation of self-expression. Considering this perspective expands one's comprehension of the potential purpose in various life stages. It exemplifies the most elementary manifestation of the means by which one might effectuate constructive transformations in one's own life and exert influence upon the global sphere.

Moreover, the choice of verbs associated with one's Ikigai may vary in accordance with shifts in personal circumstances. As an illustration, in the scenario where an individual finds themselves in an unfavorable employment situation with little prospects for resignation, one may perceive their Ikigai as the pursuit of perseverance. Every morning upon awakening to commence one's job routine, individuals often engage in a mental exercise wherein they consciously reinforce their primary goal or purpose, namely, to exhibit perseverance throughout this specific phase of their existence. In a professional setting, individuals have the opportunity to employ various coping mechanisms aimed at enhancing their capacity for patience and tolerance. In addition to professional settings, individuals have the opportunity to cultivate constructive behaviors that align with the concept of perseverance in their personal lives, such as engaging in athletic activities or enrolling in educational programs of limited duration. Through this process, one has the ability to transform a flawed Ikigai into a purposeful Ikigai, without necessitating a complete life redesign.

2 - An Exploration of Social Anxiety

Social anxiety disorder, commonly referred to as SAD, has been documented throughout history, dating back to prehistoric times. During the early 1900s, the condition commonly referred to as "social phobia" underwent a change in nomenclature and was subsequently labeled as "social neurosis" in the following decades. During the 1960s, the American Psychiatric Association recognized and classified this condition as a disorder, granting it official recognition and approval for inclusion in the list of recognized illnesses. The subject in question did not garner significant attention until the post-1980s era, and its prevalence is more widespread than previously acknowledged. Anxiety disorder, a highly distressing ailment, affects a significant number of individuals worldwide, with millions experiencing its debilitating effects on a daily basis. Certain individuals may experience this phenomenon due to a particular form of social anxiety, while others may have a more broad-based manifestation.

Social anxiety is a ubiquitous aspect of human existence and holds significance in the early stages of childhood development. However, when an individual experiences persistent and enduring worry in social environments, it is classified as a mental disease. A positive association has been observed indicating a familial tendency for social anxiety. Nevertheless, the underlying cause of this phenomenon remains uncertain, as it is unclear if it is attributable to genetic predisposition or the child's home environment. The presence of highly domineering or authoritarian parents who impose strict standards of perfection can potentially lead to the development of Social Anxiety Disorder (SAD).

The prevalence of social anxiety disorder varies between cultures, as certain societies stigmatize introversion, whereas others embrace it as a socially acceptable trait. In the context of the United States, there appears to be a preference for those who exhibit extroverted traits, hence placing an additional strain on individuals who identify as introverts. In instances where Seasonal Affective Disorder (SAD) is identified, it is typically observed to manifest throughout adolescence. The occurrence of this condition in individuals during their later stages of life is highly uncommon.

Based on studies conducted in the United States, social anxiety disorder has been identified as the third most prevalent psychiatric disorder, ranking below alcoholism and depression. The findings of this research suggest that around 7% of the population presently experiences some manifestation of social anxiety disorder. Other countries exhibit varying figures, with England, for instance, demonstrating a mere 0.4%, while India displays a rate of 12.8%. The United States is positioned in the higher range of the spectrum. The prevalence statistic in the United States indicates that around one in every 14 individuals within one's social network experiences this illness.

If an individual's Facebook friends list comprises 140 individuals, it can be inferred that approximately 10 of their friends are afflicted with anxiety condition. This information alone should facilitate your comprehension that you are not the sole being in existence. There are individuals that have a similar predicament to yours and have acquired efficient strategies to properly cope with it.

Individuals who experience social anxiety are sometimes characterized as exhibiting a pronounced inclination towards shyness. It is a common experience for individuals to occasionally experience feelings of shyness or nervousness, although certain individuals may exhibit these emotions to a greater extent. For individuals belonging to this demographic, the impact can be quite incapacitating. The aforementioned circumstance has a direct impact on individuals' capacity to engage in social activities, establish new connections, and participate in novel experiences. It could potentially impede their capacity to attend employment or educational institutions.

This particular cohort is frequently categorized as introverts in contrast to extroverts. Historically, there has been a prevailing belief that a mere 25% of the United States populace identified as introverts. However, an examination conducted in the latter part of the 1990s revealed that the actual proportion is more closely approximated at 50%. The prevalence of extroversion is frequently perceived to be higher due to the tendency of introverts to conceal their true nature by adopting extroverted behaviors. Despite experiencing significant discomfort in social situations, individuals are capable of projecting a confident demeanor and appearing to others as being extroverted, despite their inherent shyness.

Various situations can elicit feelings of social anxiety, including but not limited to: public speaking, interacting with individuals in positions of authority, engaging in conversations with groups of people or even with an individual, dining in public settings, participating in performance-based activities, experiencing criticism or teasing, being the focal point of attention, navigating interpersonal relationships (romantic or otherwise), being observed while engaged in activities, engaging in phone conversations, initiating conversations with unfamiliar individuals, and discussing personal matters with others.

Individuals diagnosed with social anxiety disorder may exhibit a range of symptoms when confronted with challenging social situations. These symptoms primarily manifest as physical discomfort and may include sensations such as a fluttering sensation in the abdominal region, rapid heartbeat, excessive perspiration, facial flushing, and occasional nausea. Additionally, individuals may experience dryness in the mouth and throat, trembling, difficulty swallowing, muscle twitches primarily in the facial area, dizziness, fainting, an inability to articulate words, restlessness, stuttering, and an overwhelming sense of fear.

Individuals may experience concerns around the potential observation of their circumstances by others, leading to unfavorableattitudes and unjust evaluations being directed towards them.

The most straightforward manner to articulate the subjective experience of an individual with social anxiety disorder is to characterize it as a sensation of being under the scrutiny of others, subjected to undue attention, and harboring a pervasive belief that they are universally perceived in a negative light. Consider the implications of living one's life burdened by such thoughts. The persistent belief that one is constantly the center of attention and subject to inspection, even during mundane activities such as walking, chatting, standing, and sitting, can result in significant levels of stress.

Individuals with social anxiety commonly hold the belief that they lack competence in social contexts, perceiving themselves as uninteresting and devoid of meaningful contributions to interpersonal interactions or discussions. Following their participation in a social gathering, individuals tend to critically analyze the occasion, emphasizing and fixating solely on aspects in which they perceive their performance to be subpar. The condition exhibits a peculiar amalgamation of feelings of self-importance and feelings of inadequacy. The individual exhibits a paradoxical state of being wherein they possess a strong sense of pride, desiring to maintain a positive perception from others. However, they consistently subject themselves to feelings of humiliation by harboring the belief that they lack value, perceiving their ideas, conversation, and physical appearance as being inferior in some manner.

During adolescence, Social Anxiety Disorder (SAD) commonly presents as heightened concern with one's physical appearance in social contexts. The societal expectation to conform to specific appearance and attire standards is particularly experienced by adolescent females, although it is also evident among males. The experience of peer pressure and adherence to social norms among certain adolescents frequently results in the development of significant anxiety and, in some cases, the manifestation of nutritional disorders such as anorexia nervosa and bulimia nervosa.

The perception of constant scrutiny by others contributes to the tendency of individuals with Social Anxiety Disorder (SAD) to avoid public spaces and social engagements whenever possible. If individuals are required to participate, they will deliberately avoid attracting attention and instead remain inconspicuous, attempting to stay in the background.

The implementation of relaxation strategies has been widely recognized as an effective approach for managing stress and promoting overall well-being. These strategies encompass a

Learning techniques for achieving physical relaxation is frequently a valuable component of therapeutic interventions. Both shallow breathing and muscle tightness have been found to be associated with worry and stress. It is vital to bear in mind somatic experiences and engage in regular exercises to facilitate the acquisition of relaxation techniques. The practice of calm breathing entails the intentional deceleration of one's respiration rate. In contrast, the Progressive Muscle technique involves systematically contracting and releasing various muscle groups. Similar to other skills, the efficacy of relief measures increases when they are practiced more frequently and consistently. Additional beneficial relaxing techniques encompass practices such as meditation, massage therapy, yoga, and attentiveness to tranquil melodies. Nevertheless, it is crucial to acknowledge that the objective of relaxation is not to eradicate or evade anxiety, as anxiety is not entirely perilous. Rather, the purpose is to facilitate the endurance of these emotions.

Coping with Negative Cognition

Do you tend to have a pessimistic outlook, perceiving the glass as half empty? Do you observe a consistent pattern among those who tend to wake up and start their day with a positive attitude? During the commute, it is probable that one will come to a halt at red traffic signals rather than proceeding through yellow signals. This is a more convenient option compared to navigating through the traffic lane. There is a moderate likelihood that the individual will be positioned on the left side while traveling in the right direction.

When engaged in a state of discontent, do you find yourself yearning to be the individual that traverses beneath the cumulonimbus clouds throughout the entirety of the day? Do you have a growing sensation of isolation and exclusion as your more cheerful colleagues actively avoid you, treating you as if you were contagious? As one reflects upon their daily experiences while returning home and contemplates the congested traffic before retiring for the night, a thought arises: would one's fortunes be nonexistent in the absence of misfortune?

If there is something in this statement that resonates with you, it is important to understand that self-limiting beliefs and acts do not necessarily have to be permanently debilitating. The psychological and emotional states of self-defeat, in which an individual has developed a compulsive and physiological dependence, do not necessarily have to exert control over or define one's life.

It is possible that you have encountered DVDs such as "The Key" or "What the Bleep We Know?" It is possible that you have assimilated a substantial amount of self-help literature. The individual in question engages in consistent practice of affirmations and meditation; nonetheless, they continue to seek fulfillment or satisfaction. Over the course of a few days or weeks, there will be no alteration to your cognitive processes and behavioral patterns.

What are the issues or problems that exist in the world? The challenge is in the intricate process of harmonizing one's ideas and emotions with acquired facts and knowledge, so facilitating the cultivation of desired interpersonal connections through the mere adaptation of one's expectations. Nevertheless, even with a comprehensive understanding of the learned experience, and firmly acknowledging its accuracy and validity, there appears to be a limitation in effectively incorporating and utilizing it to bring about constructive and enduring transformation.

The information and knowledge that one frequently endeavors to apply in their lives are indeed valid. By altering our mental patterns, we can enhance our productivity, personal growth, and overall satisfaction. This phenomenon is clearly observed in a multitude of biographical accounts as well as in a myriad of narratives depicting the achievements of ordinary individuals who have seemingly surmounted insurmountable challenges. The unavailability of the experience might be attributed to the insufficiency and inherent flaws in the offered evidence and suggested methodologies.

Before delving further into this issue, allow me to present a selection of noteworthy research and development endeavors conducted in this particular discipline. NeuroVector Neuroscience Laboratories is a privately-owned research facility located in Melbourne, Australia. The research center is located in a suburb that is next to Western Sydney University and is in close proximity to three of Australia's leading neurotechnology research universities. Additionally, they maintain regular communication with universities and research institutions both domestically in the United States and internationally, in order to stay updated on the latest discoveries and advancements in technology.

The researchers' work has made a substantial contribution to the development of a pioneering neurovector brainwave synchronization audio technology. When utilized as instructed, this technology has been shown to produce notable and enduring enhancements in the structure and functioning of the nervous system. Extensive testing has been conducted on the breakthrough neuroVector technology, demonstrating its operational functionality for all users. They provide an absolute assurance that your life will undergo a profound transformation that will consistently astonish you.

During the course of their investigation, the laboratory personnel identified a neurological defect that hinders an individual's ability to effectively comprehend and implement the basic principles and methodologies presented by different authors. When a someone recalls an experience with a positive attitude, they are more likely to remember just the positive aspects and, consequently, the most significant milestones. The human mind sometimes conflates present thoughts and perceptions with memories of former events, leading to a misleading sense of comfort and simplicity that does not accurately reflect the unique nature of the current experience.

Individuals often encounter challenges when attempting tasks that they previously believed they had effortlessly mastered. This phenomenon frequently occurs due to individuals' desire for the task to be perceived as straightforward as it currently appears. The brain serves as a repository for memories, encompassing both positive and negative experiences. However, upon recollection, our access to these memories is limited to the aspects that align with our current emotional state and objectives.

The NeuroVector TREA technology has been developed by researchers and developers as a means of streamlining the intricate and advanced process of cultivating a winner's mindset in a practical and effective manner. The utilization of neuroVector TRAE's audio technology results in a synchronization of the brain's electrical activity with that of persons who have dedicated significant time and effort towards enhancing their level of consciousness.

Cognitive Disengagement From Negative Thinking

Given the notable achievements you have attained thus far, it is evident that you have developed certain areas of proficiency and acquired heightened fortitude in confronting circumstances that typically elicit avoidance or trigger anxiety. After eliminating superfluous items from your lists, it becomes more feasible to concentrate on the remaining issues that require your attention. Throughout the course of this week, it is recommended that individuals allocate their attention towards the following daily activities: • Engage in the act of perusing an extensive compilation of noteworthy materials, with the suggested frequency of 2-3 instances per day.

- Document your levels of anxiety and track your progress.

- Enumerate hypothetical concerns.

- Engage in the practice of journaling to document expressions of gratitude.

On the fifteenth day

Select an alternative weekly objective that is relevant to a concern that exacerbates your anxiety. If one happens to possess none remaining, commendations are in order. Nevertheless, identify an aspect of your life that you would like to enhance. Outline the necessary steps to achieve your weekly objective and select one of those tasks to commence today.

Engage in a leisurely stroll within the vicinity of your residential area or explore an unfamiliar setting to introduce a novel visual environment. Engage in ambulation spanning a minimum distance of 8 city blocks. When encountering individuals during your stroll, it is advisable to exhibit a friendly gesture by smiling and inquiring about their well-being. In the event of a non-response, it is advisable to adopt a nonchalant attitude, refraining from taking any offense on a personal level.

One may engage in a period of meditation lasting 30 minutes in order to achieve a state of relaxation at a later time. During this period, it is advisable to engage in positive thinking by focusing solely on envisioning favorable events in one's life. Envision a scenario in which one successfully surmounts all personal challenges and attains the liberty to pursue endeavors without the influence of anxiety impeding their overall well-being and contentment.

On the sixteenth day

Today, endeavor to address a theoretical concern as your objective. For example, in the event that one considers a pessimistic situation, such as the occurrence of a card decline despite the knowledge of sufficient funds in one's account, it may be advisable to simulate such a scenario. While it is not recommended to attempt purchasing items that are unavailable at a store or smoothie shop, individuals who are inclined to undertake such a challenge may do so, provided that they refrain from engaging in any form of theft. Please construct a hypothetical scenario and articulate the probable outcome. For example, in the event that an individual is unable to provide payment at the point of sale, they will be unable to complete the transaction. There will be no legal action taken against you.

Occasionally, individuals may generously offer food items without charge as an act of kindness. There exists a multitude of alternative scenarios that can be constructed to align with one's hypothetical concerns.

Select three musical compositions for the purpose of either engaging in a dance performance or vocal rendition today. If one engages in the act of dancing, it is advisable to exert maximum effort and enthusiasm in order to fully express oneself. In the event that one engages in vocal performance, it is advised to exert maximal effort and express oneself with great passion and intensity. It is anticipated that one's neighbors will perceive auditory stimuli emitted by oneself. Subsequently, locate a comedic motion picture to view prior to retiring for the night.

On the seventeenth day.

Consider an additional hypothetical concern and propose a potential solution to mitigate it. The concerns in question can manifest in diverse forms, necessitating a creative approach, akin to the previous day's objective. To cultivate a positive emotional state, it is recommended to engage in the pen exercise once more. In this instance, I suggest extending the duration from 5 minutes to 7 minutes. Engage in a 30-minute yoga session at some point during the day, followed by allocating a separate period for leisurely reading, aiming to cover a minimum of 30 pages from a preferred literary work.

The Mechanisms Underlying Fear

The experience of strange or irrational fear can be attributed to the influence of negative reasoning, specifically worry, that arises from anxiety. This anxiety is characterized by an abstract sense of misgiving or fear. The phenomenon of irrational fear follows a common neural pathway characterized by various apprehensions. This pathway is intricately connected to the nervous system, enabling the activation of bodily resources in response to potential dangers or risks. A considerable number of individuals experience fear in relation to phenomena or circumstances that are unfamiliar or not readily understood. This unfounded phobia can extend to various domains, such as the realm of the unknown, the forthcoming decade, or even the immediate future. The persistent and irrational fear has detrimental consequences as the triggering stimulus is frequently absent or perceived through fantasies. The presence of such fear may contribute to the comorbidity within the broader spectrum of anxiety disorders. The emotion of fear can lead individuals to anticipate and anticipate potential future threats, rather than engaging in proactive planning and evaluation of potential outcomes. Many educators perceive the pursuit of further academic knowledge as a potential risk, leading to feelings of apprehension and stress. Consequently, they may prioritize teaching familiar subjects they are already knowledgeable about, rather than engaging in new areas of research. This can potentially elicit certain behaviors, such as idleness and procrastination.

The prevalence of anxiety is often higher in certain populations, particularly those who are consistently exposed to uncertain and unpredictable circumstances, such as individuals residing in war-torn areas or regions characterized by conflict, terrorism, and abuse. Inadequate parental upbringing that instills fear can also hinder a child's cognitive development and personality development. For example, parents provide guidance to their children, advising them against engaging in conversations with individuals who are not part of their immediate social circle, with the intention of ensuring their safety and protection. In an educational setting, students are often encouraged to exhibit confidence and assertiveness when engaging in conversations with individuals outside of their immediate social circle. However, they are also advised to exercise caution and be mindful of potential risks and the context in which these interactions take place. Ambiguous and mixed signals of this nature have the potential to impact an individual's level of confidence and self-assurance. Scholars argue that engaging in conversations with individuals outside of one's immediate social circle should not be discouraged, but rather encouraged within the context of a parent's presence, if deemed necessary. The cultivation of a sense of tranquility as a means of coping with diverse circumstances is often advocated as a remedy for irrational fear and as a foundational skill by various ancient philosophies.

Species-specific defense reactions (SSDRs) or avoidance The phenomenon of learning in nature refers to the specific tendency of organisms to avoid certain risks, thereby ensuring their survival within natural environments. Both humans and animals exhibit species-specific defense responses, such as the flight-or-fight response. These responses also encompass pseudo-aggression, which refers to the display of fake or intimidating aggression, as well as the freeze reaction to perceived threats. These defense mechanisms are regulated by the sympathetic nervous system. The acquisition of these social and self-directed learning behaviors occurs expeditiously via social interactions among conspecifics, heterospecifics, and exposure to the surrounding environment. The acquired sets of responses or reactions are not readily disregarded. The animal that exhibits resilience is the one that possesses a clear understanding of potential threats and possesses the ability to effectively evade such dangers. In individuals, a common behavioralpattern is observed when encountering a snake, wherein many individuals instinctively retreat before consciously recognizing the nature of the stimulus, occasionally mistaking it for an innocuous object such as a stick.

Similarly, within the realm of cognitive processes, various regions of the cerebral cortex are involved in the neural processing of fear in both humans and other nonhuman organisms. The amygdala establishes connections with several brain regions, including the prefrontal cortex, hypothalamus, sensory cortex, hippocampus, thalamus, septum, and brainstem. The amygdala plays a crucial role in the phenomenon known as stimulus-specific defensive response (SSDR). One important component of this process is the ventral amygdalofugal pathway, which is essential for associative learning. SSDRs are acquired through the association of stimuli with the environment and conspecifics. An emotional response occurs following the transmission of signals among different regions of the brain, which subsequently activates the sympathetic nervous system. This system is responsible for regulating the flight, fight, freeze, fear, and blackout responses. Frequently, an impaired amygdala can result in a diminished ability to recognize and respond to fear, potentially leading to a state of disability. This impediment can result in a lack of fear response in different species, often leading to excessive confidence, such as confronting larger peers or approaching aggressive animals.

In his study conducted in 1970, Robert C. Bolles, a researcher affiliated with the

University of Washington, sought to investigate species-specific defense reactions and avoidance learning in various animals. Bolles discovered that the theories surrounding avoidance learning and the methods employed to measure this propensity were disconnected from real-world contexts. The researcher postulated the existence of a species-specific defense reaction (SSDR). There exist three distinct categories of stress response known as SSDRs, namely flight, fight (also referred to as pseudo-aggression), and freeze. Undoubtedly, even domesticated animals exhibit spontaneous self-directed responses (SSDRs), during which they revert to ancestral instincts and manifest a state of "wildness" once again. According to Dr.Bolles, reactions are consistently dependent on the reinforcement of a safety signal, rather than the aversive conditioned stimuli. This security sign has the potential to serve as a valuable source of input or facilitate opportunities for improvement and change. Internal criticism or information, such as muscle jerks and heightened pulse, is considered to be more influential in self-selected deep relaxation (SSDR) than external input, which comes from the surrounding environment. According to Dr.Bolles' research, it has been observed that a significant number of animal species possess inherent patterns of fear, which serve as a mechanism to ensure the survival of their respective populations. Rodents exhibit a tendency to rapidly retreat from any perceived threat, while pigeons demonstrate an increased wing flapping frequency in response to compromised situations. The phenomenon of wing fluttering in pigeons and the evasive running behavior observed in rodents are considered to be defense mechanisms or behavioral adaptations unique to each species. Bolles acknowledged that the formation of specific stimulus-stimulus response (SSDR) associations occurs primarily through Pavlovian conditioning rather than operant conditioning. SSDRs arise as a result of the interplay between ecological stimuli and aversive events. An examination was conducted by Michael S. Fanselow to investigate specific defense responses. It was observed that rodents exposed to two different shock conditions exhibited contrasting reactions based on instinct or spatial awareness, rather than scientific knowledge.

Interpersonal Communication In Romantic Relationships

Effective communication skills can significantly impact the success or failure of one's romantic relationships. This analysis will examine the influence of proficient or deficient communication skills on interpersonal relationships.

Being proficient in communication entails the ability to engage in active and effective listening.

One should engage in the practice of introspection by closely examining their own thoughts and emotions.

3. Acquire the ability to discern situations where a response is unnecessary.

One effective strategy for developing empathy is to engage in the observation of individuals and subsequently engage in the practice of empathy.

In order to generate thoughtful and suitable responses, it is imperative to engage in introspection and observation of both oneself and others, employing empathy as a guiding principle.

By possessing the capability to perform these tasks, one is able to establish a profound connection with individuals by means of comprehension. One possesses the capacity to proficiently disseminate information to others and also acquire information in a reciprocal manner. These five points have been found to be advantageous in various types of relationships. Interpersonal relationships are fundamentally predicated on establishing and maintaining connections, which can prove challenging in the absence of effective communication skills.

Individuals who encounter challenges in effective communication may experience difficulties in engaging with others in both professional and personal contexts. Achieving mutual understanding in interpersonal relationships can be significantly challenging if one lacks the ability to actively listen to others and effectively communicate their thoughts and feelings verbally. The ability to introspect and articulate one's thoughts and emotions, whether through written or oral expression, holds significant importance. Conversely, a lack of proficiency in this domain can contribute to interpersonal miscommunications and misunderstandings within relationships.

Instances of ineffective communication are not solely limited to the exchange of harsh language or the escalation of vocal tones. In the majority of instances, ineffective communication can be attributed to a deficiency in communication. When certain aspects are left unacknowledged or unexpressed, individuals tend to make assumptions about each other, leading to the formation of conclusions. To mitigate the occurrence of ineffective communication within relationships, it is advisable to employ a strategy of excessive communication. Through the act of extensively conveying one's intentions and thoughts, the recipient gradually develops an understanding of the communicator's communication style and cognitive processes. The greater their understanding of the cognitive processes occurring within your mind, the reduced likelihood of misinterpreting your intentions or actions.

This holds particular significance during the initial stages of relationships, as it is during this period that individuals encounter the most substantial learning curve. This assertion is applicable not solely to romantic relationships, but also extends to professional, personal, and familial relationships. Similar to the likelihood of possessing a comprehensive comprehension of the cognitive and communicative patterns exhibited by one's closest confidant, it is imperative to acknowledge the limited grasp one may possess regarding the cognitive and emotional processes of a recently acquainted colleague, and vice versa. To mitigate the occurrence of misunderstandings and disputes, it is imperative to engage in thorough and extensive communication, thereby eliminating any potential for misinterpretations. Once a mutual understanding has been established between individuals, they can collaboratively establish a unique mode of communication that is effective for both parties involved.

The Individual Ascribes His Achievements To A Multitude Of Factors.

The concept of folding early entails the act of departing from a situation when it begins to deteriorate, without attempting to salvage it. It emphasizes the acceptance that once something is irretrievably lost, it is futile to exert efforts towards its recovery.

Engage in daily reading as a means of fostering a lifelong commitment to self-directed learning. Foster a sense of curiosity and actively pursue personal growth by striving to expand one's knowledge incrementally each day.

Strive to engage in swimming with a competitive mindset, disregarding the influence of tides. In the face of adversity, persevere and maintain unwavering determination.

It is advisable to implement the knowledge acquired and refrain from concerning oneself with the opinions or actions of others.

Exhibiting aggressive behavior in response to being presented with an opportunity.

Adhering to appropriate conduct is imperative in order to mitigate the risk of succumbing to irrational patterns of thought and behavior, which could potentially yield adverse consequences in subsequent periods.

By identifying investment opportunities that are currently priced below their intrinsic value and possess significant potential for generating financial returns.

Charlie Munger's approach involves identifying and comprehending the fundamental concepts, known as mental models, derived from the fields of physics, economics, and psychology, and subsequently integrating them into one's everyday existence.

The significance of reading lies in its inherent value and numerous benefits.

Engaging in reading activities facilitates the acquisition of knowledge and understanding pertaining to various subjects that would otherwise remain unfamiliar in the absence of reading books or magazines. Reading serves as a catalyst for personal growth, enabling individuals to experience moments of enlightenment, derive motivation, and generate novel ideas applicable to their plans, businesses, and other endeavors. The act of reading can serve as a guiding framework for achieving one's objectives. A blueprint, which entails a comprehensive plan outlining the necessary steps to accomplish a particular task, can be likened to the insights and knowledge gained through reading. Literary works possess the potential to significantly impact individuals' lives, serving as a means of solace and escape from distressing circumstances. For instance, religious texts such as the Bible have been recognized for their ability to provide solace and guidance. Similarly, the field of psychology offers a range of books that can offer comparable benefits, aiding individuals in navigating challenging situations and fostering personal growth. The inclusion of these entities can enhance the quality of one's life. Various subjects such as business, health, fitness, investing, and cooking encompass a wide range of knowledge that can be explored and understood through the act of reading and problem-solving.

The selection of reading material holds significant importance, particularly in the realm of self-improvement, where the recommended genre encompasses self-help literature. Psychological literature explores the intricate relationship between financial matters and human behavior. It is crucial to acknowledge that the information one assimilates into their cognitive faculties significantly influences subsequent outcomes. This principle extends beyond the realm of finance and encompasses the domains of health and fitness as well. Engaging in reading activities fosters a deeper comprehension and appreciation of these subjects. Books have the potential to enhance one's personal growth by fostering creativity, confidence, and imagination. Additionally, they contribute to the development of verbal skills, thereby increasing one's competitiveness in a highly competitive society. Reading can serve as a form of meditation and a means of detachment from reality. By immersing oneself in a novel, individuals can not only gain knowledge about the trials faced by characters, but also acquire wisdom on how to overcome challenging circumstances. This, I contend, should be the primary motivation for engaging with works of fiction.

Indeed, individuals such as Warren Buffet, Tony Robbins, Oprah Winfrey, Steve Jobs, and numerous other affluent billionaires and millionaires allocate time to engage in reading activities and actively promote the habit of daily reading. Warren Buffet, a prominent figure in the business world and a close associate of Charlie Munger, possesses a substantial net worth of $75.6 billion, making him the second wealthiest individual in the United States. In this book, I will delve further into Buffet's accomplishments. When queried about the factors contributing to his remarkable achievements, Buffet gestured towards a collection of books in close proximity and emphasized the significance of reading 500 pages daily. The accumulation of knowledge can be likened to the compounding effect of interest.

The act of reading has significantly contributed to my intellectual growth, fostering an enhanced cognitive capacity. Moreover, it has instilled within me a sense of self-assurance, discouraging any self-doubt. Reading has also honed my critical thinking skills, allowing me to perceive perceived adversities in my life as valuable resources that can be leveraged to my benefit. Consequently, this newfound perspective has propelled me forward in my endeavor to author this book.

The Field Of Epidemiology Investigates The Prevalence And Determinants Of Borderline Personality Disorder.

Hippocrates and Homer provided explanations for the presence of a range of intense and diverse emotional states, including impulsive anger, mania, and depression, which are characteristic of borderline personality disorder. The term in question experienced a resurgence in the latter part of the 17th century, as Swiss physician TheophileBonet reintroduced it to elucidate the occurrence of emotional instability coupled with an unpredictable nature. The term "borderline" was originally introduced by Adolf Stern in 1938 to describe a cohort of patients who exhibited symptoms that he believed represented a milder form of schizophrenia, characterized by a borderline state between psychosis and neurosis. The condition was given its name due to the presence of borderline symptoms in patients.

Approximately 35% of individuals diagnosed with borderline personality disorder achieve remission as a result of their treatment. Multiple studies have observed that a significant proportion, exceeding 86%, of individuals diagnosed with borderline personality disorder can attain a state of enduring recovery through the implementation of extended therapeutic interventions. Contrary to prevailing popular beliefs, individuals diagnosed with borderline personality disorder have the potential to achieve recovery, even in the face of severe symptoms.

Epidemiology is a branch of medical science that focuses on the study of the distribution

The incidence of borderline personality disorder is estimated to range from 1% to 2% among individuals in the general population. Furthermore, it has been observed that women exhibit a higher propensity for developing borderline personality disorder compared to men, potentially attributed to the presence of an excess of the hormone estrogen. According to a study conducted in 2008, the prevalence of borderline personality disorder was shown to be 5.6% in males and 6.2% in women. Nevertheless, certain experts argue that the prevalence rate of borderline personality disorder is insignificant.

This specific personality disorder is believed to account for a minimum of 20% of psychiatric admissions. Additionally, this condition is responsible for 10% of outpatient psychiatric consultations in the United States.

Conversely, the borderline personality disorder is a prevalent condition that has affected incarcerated individuals nationwide. The prevalence of borderline personality disorder within the prison population in the United States is estimated to be 17%. The elevated prevalence of individuals incarcerated in United States prisons can be attributed to the heightened frequency of prisoners who are affected by substance abuse and mood disorders.

As previously stated, individuals diagnosed with borderline personality disorder have the potential to achieve recovery from their condition. Nevertheless, the process of recovery may be arduous due to the overwhelming surge of emotions experienced by the individual undergoing treatment. While it is true that individuals afflicted with this condition have the capacity to maintain regular and healthy lifestyles. The subsequent section outlines the various treatment and management strategies that are accessible for individuals afflicted with borderline personality disorder.

1: The Correlation between Proper Breathing and Optimal Health

In addition to proper nutrition, adopting a healthy lifestyle, and engaging in physical exercise, optimal respiratory practices play a crucial role in attaining overall well-being. Nevertheless, a significant portion of individuals endure the entirety of their lifetimes managing stress, anxiety, depression, and other associated health ailments due to their lack of knowledge regarding proper breathing techniques.

This provides an overview of various techniques and strategies for proper breathing.

What is the process of respiration in humans?

Breathing is commonly regarded as an involuntary physiological process that sustains human life. This assertion holds true, as the cessation of respiration would inevitably compromise one's vitality.

Respiration is a continuous process that facilitates the intake of essential oxygen into the human body while simultaneously eliminating carbon dioxide. In contrast to processes such as digestion or the cardiac cycle, respiration is a physiological function that humans possess the ability to consciously regulate.

Can you recall the act of engaging in deep breathing exercises during episodes of panic attacks? Have you ever experienced a sensation of breathlessness following the ascent of multiple flights of stairs, necessitating a period of slow and deep inhalations until your respiration returned to a steady state?

These instances provide evidence that individuals have the ability to regulate their breathing in order to manage various experiences. This implies that individuals have the ability to exert control over their bodies in order to promote overall well-being. Directing attention towards one's breath can lead to improved mental and emotional well-being, facilitating the management of conditions such as depression, stress, anxiety, and various other emotional states.

The act of breathing is often overlooked by individuals, possibly due to its innate nature within the human body. You use your breath in many ways daily: you breathe deeply when you are laughing aloud, you hyperventilate when you feel panic or fear, and you grasp when you are crying.

However, many people live day-to-day with shallow and unconscious breaths – which is a not a good recipe for good health. Many people do not realize that they are not breathing right. Some doctors say that the breathing pattern of many people indicates stress and anxiety most of the time.

When you breathe this way, you are sending a message to your nervous system that you are indeed stressed, so it becomes a cycle.

How to Properly Breathe

To know what proper breathing is all about, doctors suggest observing a newborn baby or your pet while they are sleeping – you'll see that their breathing is slow, steady, and effortless, coming from their stomachs.

During infancy, the individual had appropriate respiratory patterns; nevertheless, once reaching the age of four or five, they developed suboptimal breathing behaviours. It is probable that individuals have engaged in suboptimal breathing patterns for a significant portion of their lives by the time they commemorate their 40th birthday.

Despite the potential for change, individuals seeking to enhance their respiratory well-being and achieve better health must be willing to challenge long-held beliefs and adopt significant modifications to their lifestyle.

The initial action to undertake is directing one's focus towards the process of respiration. Develop an awareness of one's respiration patterns during periods of heightened stress, states of happiness, engaging in sexual activity, or engaging in physical exercise. Once an individual comprehends the mechanics of respiration, initiating modifications becomes more feasible.

The act of respiration holds significant importance in the practise of yoga and various meditation techniques. In fact, it surpasses the significance of mastering the physical postures typically associated with these practises.

In Sanskrit, the term for breath is prana, which is translated as energy. This serves as a significant measure of one's whole state of welfare. Therefore, engaging in activities such as yoga, tai chi, and Pilates that emphasise breath control can serve as effective starting points for acquiring healthy breathing techniques.

The Correlation Between Pet Ownership And Mental Well-Being

In addition to the aforementioned advantages, pets exert a direct influence on mental well-being.

1. The presence of pets has been found to potentially mitigate symptoms of depression.

Depression, in its most basic form, can be characterised as a profound state of isolation. Individuals experiencing depression require assistance in redirecting their cognitive attention towards positive aspects. Rearing pets is considered to be one of the most effective methods for enhancing mental well-being.

Numerous individuals have a profound sense of accomplishment in their life via the act of nurturing and tending to their dogs. Individuals encounter a state of calmness and discover a sense of meaning.

Pets have the potential to enhance an individual's sociability.

Engaging in dog walking activities can facilitate interpersonal communication. While strolling in the park with your canine companions, it is likely that you may encounter fellow individuals who are also accompanied by their pets. Consequently, the probability of establishing new social connections is elevated. Increased social contacts and relationships have been found to be associated with improved overall well-being.

The act of raising a pet not only contributes to personal happiness but also serves to safeguard the wellbeing of the animals involved.

It is advisable to maintain distance from individuals who are experiencing high levels of stress.

According to a new study, the presence of individuals experiencing high levels of stress can exert a notable influence on the structural composition of the human brain. This phenomenon may account for the observation that family members of individuals with depression frequently exhibit similar symptoms to those experienced by the depressed individual.

Furthermore, the study provides additional support for the assertion made by certain experts that individuals with negative attitudes have the potential to influence others in a detrimental manner. The study revealed that stress has a significant impact not just on individuals' emotional well-being but also on their bodily functioning.

Dr. Toni-Lee Sterley, the primary author of the aforementioned study, articulated a remarkable finding. Sterley (year) elucidated that previous literature has demonstrated the phenomenon of stress transfer, however our study provides evidence that the brain undergoes alterations as a result of such transferred stress.

What are the effects on the brain when individuals are exposed to individuals experiencing stress? According to Sterley, the researchers observed that the neurons responsible for regulating the brain's reaction to stress exhibited similar alterations in unstressed couples as those observed in stressed mice.

This study contributes to the expanding corpus of scientific literature indicating that engaging with individuals who are experiencing depression may have adverse effects. Avoiding persons who are experiencing high levels of stress can be a beneficial course of action. However, it is vital to ascertain the indicators of stress in an individual.

Stressed individuals commonly exhibit recurring behaviours. The following are few indicators that an individual is experiencing high levels of stress.

1. Excessive disclosure of personal issues

Expressing one's emotions can be beneficial in certain situations. Indeed, it may be argued that this particular therapeutic approach is among the most efficacious. Engaging in conversation with a companion can effectively alleviate internal distress.

However, those experiencing high levels of stress engage in this behaviour to an excessive degree. The individuals in question exhibit a tendency to disproportionately emphasise their adverse encounters. Furthermore, the act of storytelling has the potential to persist indefinitely. Individuals often encounter challenges when attempting to release negative previous experiences.

Many individuals exhibit a tendency to excessively concern themselves with matters beyond their sphere of influence.

Throughout the course of our existence, we inevitably confront many obstacles and setbacks. This phenomenon is inherent to the human condition. Individuals who are in good health possess the ability to acquire knowledge and subsequently progress without being hindered by obstacles.

However, those experiencing stress are unable to accomplish such tasks. Individuals often have a tendency to ruminate on matters that are beyond their ability to alter. Consequently, individuals sometimes find themselves confined within a self-imposed enclosure.

3. Consume nutritionally deficient meals

It is possible that you have also observed a correlation — individuals under stress often have a tendency to consume excessive quantities of food. This phenomenon elucidates why not all individuals experiencing depression exhibit a slender physique. A portion of the individuals in question exhibit a higher body mass index.

One concerning aspect is that a majority of those experiencing stress tend to consume nutritionally poor diets. Individuals often have a tendency to shift their focus towards consuming food as a means of temporarily escaping or suppressing their issues and frustrations.

The individual exhibits a tendency to experience a heightened startle response.

Individuals experiencing high levels of stress often exhibit a heightened susceptibility to becoming overwhelmed. Even relatively minor stressors have the potential to elicit significant reactions in such individuals.

Insufficient sleep is a common phenomenon experienced by individuals, particularly when their minds are preoccupied with numerous thoughts and concerns.

However, individuals experiencing high levels of stress often struggle to obtain sufficient amounts of sleep. The individual's cognitive processes are characterised by the presence of magnified pessimistic perceptions.

Engaging in multitasking

The majority of individuals engage in the practise of creating daily schedules for their routine tasks. The primary objective of scheduling is to maintain order and optimise the utilisation of time and resources.

Individuals under high levels of stress exhibit distinct behaviours and responses in comparison to others who are not under significant stress. Rather of adhering to a predetermined plan, individuals have a tendency to complete multiple things concurrently.

As anticipated, individuals experience fatigue and weariness when reaching the conclusion of the day. One drawback associated with their habitual behaviour is the frequent occurrence of errors. And self-deprecating language will persist.

7. It is not advisable to seek assistance.

Individuals who possess good health tend to seek help or support when they encounter uncertainty or lack clarity on their actions. Individuals experiencing high levels of stress tend to refrain from engaging in the activity. Individuals often exhibit a tendency to independently achieve tasks, even in situations where assistance is urgently required.

8. Emphasise the adverse aspects of an encounter.

The determining factor of a positive or negative experience lies not solely in the experience itself, but rather in the manner in which we interpret and perceive said experience. An individual who possesses rationality will direct their attention towards the favourable aspects of an occurrence, rather than fixating on the unfavourable aspects.

Individuals experiencing high levels of stress often exhibit behaviours that are contrary to what is expected or desired. Frequently, individuals tend to perceive the negative aspects rather than the positive ones. Individuals who harbour negative thoughts and perceptions tend to express themselves in a pessimistic manner.

Procrastination can be easily experienced.

At certain junctures in our existence, we experience the phenomenon of procrastination. However, individuals with a positive mindset are inclined to discover strategies to cultivate motivation.

Individuals experiencing high levels of stress may be more susceptible to feelings of discouragement when faced with unexpected outcomes, as their cognitive state is already burdened with negative thoughts and emotions. The stakeholders are first visible during the initiation phase of a project, but eventually, they will become less prominent or disappear altogether.

The individual consistently exhibits a propensity for expeditiousness.

Individuals experiencing high levels of stress often have a tendency to constantly rush or be in a state of haste. The observation reveals individuals engaging in hurried activities without achieving any significant outcomes. By the conclusion of the day, it is evident that they exhibit signs of fatigue, yet have consistently failed to complete any assigned tasks. If one observes certain attributes in an individual, it is possible that they are experiencing symptoms of stress.

In order to mitigate the potential impact, it is advisable for individuals to maintain a distance from the situation. It is advisable to prioritise one's personal goals. Ensure your safety.

The Role Of Emotional Intelligence In Interpersonal Relationships

The term 'connection' is commonly employed in the field of psychology as well as in other languages across the globe. Relationships can be described as the manner in which two or more concepts, objects, or individuals are interconnected, or the condition of being interconnected. When individuals contemplate the concept of 'relationship,' their thoughts tend to go towards the romantic kind by default. While the commonly perceived notion of relationships often revolves around a specific type, it is important to acknowledge the existence of various other relationship types. In essence, it may be condensed into four overarching categories; nevertheless, a more granular examination reveals the existence of numerous distinct relationship types, numbering in the hundreds. This will examine the dynamics of interpersonal interactions and explore the potential for enhancing them via the application of emotional intelligence.

Various Categories of Interpersonal Relationships

When considering the subject of relationships, a significant portion of individuals lack a comprehensive understanding of the matter. The initial phases of a love relationship often evoke a sense of exhilaration among the majority of individuals. However, upon resuming their customary everyday activities, individuals may encounter the manifestation of their personal issues, leading to an escalation of conflicts, emotional distress, retreat, inadequate coping mechanisms, or a sense of monotony. It is indisputable that the task of sustaining a good and contented relationship is challenging. Fortunately, there exists an expanding realm of scholarly inquiry centred on the study of interpersonal relationships and emotional intelligence. This discipline offers evidence-based strategies and recommendations for cultivating positive habits that contribute to the cultivation of optimal levels of satisfaction within partnerships. We establish interpersonal connections that encompass not only affection but also diligent effort and effective communication. In this course, we will explore the underlying principles that underlie relationships, focusing on the intricate nature of their mastery. Additionally, we will investigate the role of emotional intelligence in enhancing these connections.

Friendships are interpersonal relationships that are formed between individuals based on mutual affection, trust, and

Friendship can be defined as a profound bond between two individuals characterised by sentiments of esteem, attentiveness, solicitude, reverence, and affection. The major defining attribute of friendship can be described as the manifestation of a personal preference towards a specific individual. It is important to note that individuals belonging to diverse groups may possess distinct conceptualizations and criteria pertaining to the notion of friendship. For instance, it has been seen that young children may readily choose someone as their 'best friend' shortly after initial acquaintance, but individuals from more reticent cultures or those with introverted tendencies have reported a limited number of friendships throughout their lifetime.

The concept of friendship encompasses a range of definitions, and there is no singularly agreed-upon term that universally characterises the nature and boundaries of this interpersonal relationship. Nevertheless, the following characteristics are widely seen as being prevalent in friendships:

Both individuals exhibit a mutual inclination for maintaining consistent communication with each other. Regular contact can be defined as occurring either annually or every other day.

There exists a certain level of dedication, whether it pertains to the friendship itself or the overall welfare of both individuals involved.

● The presence of mutual trust, compassion, and concern is evident in the relationship between the two individuals. ● The two individuals exhibit shared hobbies, interests, beliefs, and opinions. ● There exists a mutual exchange of knowledge regarding each other's interests, affections, fears, and emotions. ● Both individuals express feelings of respect, love, appreciation, and admiration towards one another.

Cognitive Behavioural Therapy (Cbt) Encompasses A Technique Known As Thought Challenging.

Thought challenging is a valuable cognitive-behavioral therapy (CBT) strategy that facilitates the examination of circumstances from several perspectives, employing concrete data derived from personal experiences. The process entails confronting and questioning one's pessimistic cognitions, subsequently substituting them with more optimistic and rational perspectives. The topic in question was previously addressed in the preceding .

Typically, this methodology encompasses a tripartite process. Specifically:

The process of recognising and categorising negative thoughts

The coexistence of anxiety and negative thoughts can give rise to significant challenges and potentially result in catastrophic consequences. Individuals diagnosed with an anxiety disorder exhibit a tendency to interpret stimuli or occurrences with heightened seriousness compared to individuals without such a problem. For instance, an individual who experiences a fear of dogs may see physical contact with them as posing a significant risk to their lives. The perception of safety in approaching the dog is contingent upon the individual's adoption of a pleasant demeanour. This particular phase may present a challenge due to the complexity involved in defining one's personal fears. However, a crucial inquiry to be made is the emotional state experienced at the onset of anxiety.

This is the sole definitive method for ascertaining one's fear.

The process of challenging negative thoughts

After the identification of anxieties and negative ideas, the subsequent step involves the testing of these thoughts. Could you perhaps provide further context or specify what "this" refers to? The concept essentially entails the assessment of pessimistic cognitions. What is the underlying reason for the spontaneous occurrence of these thoughts in your mind? During this particular phase, it is imperative to critically examine the substantiation underlying these pessimistic cognitions, while also endeavouring to discern any counterproductive convictions that may contribute to the emergence of negative thoughts. One potential approach to address these cognitive patterns involves engaging in a systematic evaluation of the benefits and drawbacks associated with harbouring apprehensions or anxieties about a certain matter.

The process of substituting negative thoughts with positive ones

After engaging in the process of questioning and challenging negative beliefs, the subsequent step involves substituting these negative concepts with thoughts that are grounded in realism and positivity. If encountering difficulty, individuals may also seek solace in comforting ideas or affirmations to alleviate tension in challenging situations.

Nevertheless, the process of substituting negative thoughts with positive ones sometimes proves to be more challenging in practise than it sounds in theory. This phenomenon can be attributed to the persistence of negative thoughts, which often stem from deeply ingrained beliefs that require significant effort and resilience to overcome. Hence, the incorporation of independent practise at home is a fundamental component of cognitive behavioural therapy.

The cognitive mechanisms underlying the processing of emotions by the human brain

In addition to comprehending the primary distinctions between emotions and moods, it is vital for individuals to possess knowledge regarding the cognitive processes involved in the human brain's handling of various emotions.

Consider, as an illustrative instance, the trite adage, "someone arose with a disconcerting disposition this morning." The aforementioned phrase is employed to describe a situation in which an individual exhibits a lack of positive affect or displays feelings that are commonly associated with negativity. Conversely, the aforementioned individual may experience a subsequent day whereby they awaken feeling adequately rested, content, and invigorated without any discernible cause.

One of the primary factors contributing to this phenomenon is the influence of an individual's mood and emotions, which serve as a transient cognitive state that shapes their cognitive processes and perception of the external environment. However, it should be noted that emotions can also be influenced by daily experiences, sleep patterns, hormonal fluctuations, and even environmental factors such as weather conditions. Nevertheless, it is imperative to acknowledge that the brain also assumes a pivotal function in influencing an individual's emotional state and disposition.

The limbic system plays a pivotal role in determining an individual's emotional experiences. Numerous regions inside the human brain, situated in its most primitive components, play a key role in regulating an individual's mood and emotions. It is widely believed that these particular brain regions were among the earliest to evolve in the human species.

One notable aspect of an individual experiencing a melancholic state is the potential for enhancing one's ability to discern intricate details. However, it is mostly the experience of happy emotions that enables individuals to sustain a positive mental outlook. When an individual experiences positive affect, it has been observed to enhance their receptiveness to novel experiences, foster creativity, facilitate future-oriented thinking, and promote adaptive responses to environmental fluctuations.

The limbic system is a crucial component of the brain network responsible for the regulation of daily moods and emotions experienced by individuals. The limbic system comprises interconnected brain areas that collaborate to analyse and interpret sensory information from the external environment. For instance, when an individual experiences a state of happiness, it is plausible that their hippocampus may guide them towards a route adjacent to a body of water, as opposed to a path characterised by a more sombre ambiance.

6: Neuroplasticity and the Modification of Anxiety-Related Neural Circuitry (Comprehensive Neural Reorganisation)

The brain is considered to be the most intricate and extraordinary organ among all the components of the human body. It exhibits expedited reactions to a wide range of circumstances, hence obviating the need for conscious deliberation and enabling spontaneous answers. The human brain, however captivating, may also present challenges, particularly when its natural response triggers unwarranted dread in situations devoid of any actual threat.

The utilisation of automated responses can swiftly induce a mood of panic and lead to exaggerated reactions in situations that do not warrant such responses. These factors frequently serve as catalysts for the activation of one's anxious mental state and the occurrence of panic attacks.

Fortunately, scientific research has provided evidence supporting the feasibility of retraining the amygdala, a specific region of the brain responsible for instinctive reflexes. This concept can be referred to as a comprehensive cognitive detoxification, as it parallels the benefits of a holistic physical detoxification in enhancing one's physiological well-being. Engaging in a cognitive detoxification process can facilitate the restoration and improvement of one's mental health. The following procedure outlines the steps:

Try an exposure therapy to unlearn The fear response.

Exposure therapy has been employed as a therapeutic intervention for individuals suffering from post-traumatic stress disorder, phobias, and anxiety, with the aim of facilitating their recovery and promoting the restoration of their mental well-being. The therapeutic approach entails the construction of a fear hierarchy, wherein individuals systematically progress through increasingly anxiety-provoking scenarios.

Commence by enumerating the various factors that contribute to the onset of anxiety or panic attacks. Please arrange the items in ascending order based on their level of fearfulness. It is imperative to document even the most minute stimulus that elicits anxiety. By subjecting oneself to the most minimal stimulus, one can effectively mitigate any potential disruptions to the cognitive processes and subsequent anxious reactions.

Please consider decreasing the volume of your amygdala.

There is no need for concern as surgical intervention is not necessary. According to a study conducted by neuroscientists at Harvard University, engaging in a 30-minute meditation practise on a daily basis has been found to result in a reduction in the size of the amygdala. This reduction facilitates the dominance of the rational thinking brain. Three meditation practises have been identified as particularly effective for promoting a state of tranquilly and mental well-being.

The initial technique is referred to as "focused attention." The practise entails a profound focus on a singular entity, such as the inhalation and exhalation of breath, a specific auditory stimulus, or a particular sensory perception. The second technique, referred to as "open monitoring," facilitates the cultivation of mindfulness towards one's innermost thoughts. The cultivation of compassion is facilitated by the inclusion of a traditional Buddhist practise known as "loving kindness" as the third practise.

The comprehensive nature of the subject matter may induce feelings of being overwhelmed, which I understand.

However, it is advisable to commence with shorter meditation sessions and progressively extend the duration over time. By adopting this approach, one will observe the enhanced sustainability of their mental state.

The practise of "open monitoring" is widely regarded as a highly effective therapeutic technique that entails the mindful observation of one's emotions and thoughts. This practise serves to mitigate the inclination to be overwhelmed by anxious emotions and cognitive patterns. Here's how you can do it at home in just three steps:

Step 1: Imagine a daily situation that triggers your anxiety or cause a panic attack. Make the image as vivid and realistic as possible.

Step 2: Pay attention to your emotions. What are you feeling right at this moment? It might be a sad feeling, an unsettled stomach, chest pain, or a slight burning feeling in the torso.

Step 3: Say to yourself out loud, "These emotions are just feelings in my body that will soon go away."

It's recommended to repeat these three steps at least 10 times until the anxious feelings fade away.

The Process Of Disengaging From A Challenging Dialogue

Many individuals have encountered negative encounters with this particular type of dialogue in previous instances.

It is advisable to avoid engaging in uncomfortable discussions with an inflexible and uncompromising perspective. Prior to addressing the subject matter, Weeks suggests that individuals inquire about two fundamental queries: "What is the issue at hand? Furthermore, what is the perspective of the other individual on the issue at hand? In cases where one is uncertain about the perspective of the other individual.

Effectively managing challenging conversations necessitates the adept application of interpersonal skills and empathy. However, at its core, engaging in such dialogues demands the fortitude to proceed despite potential obstacles. As one more engages in the practise of confronting these challenges directly, one's proficiency in doing so will correspondingly improve. In instances where one is uncertain about the most effective method to undertake during a pivotal conversation, the following suggestions can serve as a helpful framework:

- It is imperative to establish clarity regarding the matter at hand.
- In order to adequately prepare for the forthcoming discussion, it is important to reflect upon two fundamental inquiries: "Precisely which behaviour is the root cause of the issue?" What is the effect of the behaviour on you, the team, or the organisation? It is imperative to attain a

condition of clarity in order to effectively express the matter at hand through concise and focused phrases. Failure to do so may result in the potential deviation from the main topic at hand during the course of the talk. The absence of emphasis on the core argument may divert the discussion and undermine one's objectives.

Understanding Your Objective

What is the intended objective of this discourse? What is the intended objective? What are the essential elements that cannot be compromised or altered? According to the English philosopher Theodore Zeldin, a fruitful discourse goes beyond mere rearrangement of existing ideas and instead generates novel perspectives and insights. Which further cards do you aspire to possess in your possession upon the culmination of this discourse? After establishing the aforementioned, devise a strategy for concluding the discourse. It is imperative to ensure that the conclusion of every discourse includes unambiguous and explicitly stated action items. What actions does the individual consent to undertake? What types of help are you dedicated to offering? What potential barriers could impede the implementation of these remedial measures? What strategies do you both concur upon implementing in order to surmount such impediments? Please arrange a subsequent meeting to assess the advancement and conclusively achieve resolution on the matter under consideration.

Developing a Mindset of Inquiry

Take a brief period to engage in introspection regarding your perspective on the given circumstances and the individual implicated. What are your preexistingassumptions or beliefs regarding the subject matter? The individual's attitude has a crucial role in shaping their subsequent reactions and interpretations of the responses provided by another person. Therefore, it is advantageous to begin such a conversation with an appropriate mindset, specifically one characterised by a disposition towards inquiry. A competent physician assesses a medical condition prior to resorting to the act of prescribing medication. This principle is equally applicable to a leader. It is advisable to adopt an open-minded approach by attentively listening to the perspectives of others before forming conclusive judgements. Despite the presence of compelling evidence that leaves no room for ambiguity, it remains incumbent upon us to afford individuals the opportunity to articulate their narrative. A competent leader demonstrates a willingness to be receptive and actively pursues a deeper understanding of the truth in various circumstances. The potential result of implementing this strategy may yield unexpected findings.

An Exposition on Pharmacological Treatments for Depression

In certain cases, treatment in isolation may prove insufficient in effectively managing a depression disorder. Medication is occasionally employed as a therapeutic intervention to alleviate symptoms associated with depression. One limitation of this approach is that medication provides only a short solution. There is no singular comprehensive remedy for this condition. If drug discontinuation occurs without addressing the underlying causes adequately, there is a high likelihood of symptom recurrence in individuals with depression.

The utilisation of medication is commonly regarded as more beneficial when employed in conjunction with a form of therapy or self-help treatment. Pharmaceutical intervention can effectively alleviate symptoms, although as previously said, addressing the underlying aetiology of one's condition remains the most efficacious approach for achieving sustained remission from depression.

It is important to note that various antidepressant medications are associated with distinct profiles of adverse effects, which, in certain instances, may outweigh their therapeutic benefits. It is vital to possess comprehensive knowledge regarding the potential risks associated with any drug that one intends to consume. The responsibility lies with the individual to assess the potential hazards in comparison to the benefits.

The majority of antidepressant medications exert their effects on neurotransmitters in the brain, with a particular focus on norepinephrine and serotonin. Certain more antidepressants target the dopamine neurotransmitters within our neural system. Over the course of time, researchers have made significant findings about the chemical components responsible for the regulation of human mood. Nevertheless, a comprehensive understanding of their operational mechanisms remains elusive.

This section will provide an overview of several antidepressant medications now accessible in the market for individuals experiencing depression.

Selective serotonin reuptake inhibitors (SSRIs) are widely recognised and contemporary pharmacological interventions for the treatment of depression. Fluoxetine (Prozac), citalopram (Celexa), sertraline (Zoloft), paroxetine (Paxil), and escitalopram (Lexapro) are among the often recommended selective serotonin reuptake inhibitors (SSRIs) for the management of depression. Furthermore, these drugs are readily accessible in generic formulations. An additional category of antidepressant medications comprises serotonin and norepinephrine reuptake inhibitors, commonly referred to as SNRIs. Two examples of medications that fall within this category are duloxetine (brand name Cymbalta) and venlafaxine (brand name Effexor).

Both SNRIs and SSRIs generally exhibit less adverse effects compared to prior generations of antidepressants. Nevertheless, it is important to note that these medications may still induce adverse effects such as nausea, headaches, sleeplessness, and jitters during the initial stages of patient usage. Frequently, these symptoms will gradually diminish over a period of time. Certain patients may experience sexual dysfunction as a side effect of these medications. However, in many cases, such issues can be effectively addressed by either transitioning to an alternative prescription or modifying the dosage regimen.

Bupropion (Wellbutrin) is a widely recognised antidepressant that is notable for its mechanism of action on the neurotransmitter dopamine. This medicine exhibits similar adverse effects to the aforementioned SNRIs and SSRIs, however with a lower likelihood of inducing sexual side effects. This antidepressant is related with an increased likelihood of seizures.

Tricyclic antidepressants are a class of antidepressant medications that have been in use for a considerable period of time. These medications possess significant potency; nonetheless, their infrequent utilisation is mostly attributed to the presence of severe adverse reactions. Individuals with pre-existing cardiac issues may experience cardiovascular effects as a result of their usage, including dizziness, weight gain, sleepiness, and xerostomia. The majority of these adverse effects can be effectively mitigated through the modification of dosage levels. Nortriptyline and imipramine are among the several tricyclic compounds available.

www.ingramcontent.com/pod-product-compliance
Lightning Source LLC
Chambersburg PA
CBHW052139110526
44591CB00012B/1784